CAPTURE YOUR

Taking the first step to awakening
the week ahead

`by

Geraldine Leyden

Dedication

I dedicate this book to my family.
My wonderful husband Paddy,
my three children; Emma, Shea and Clíodhna,
and most importantly my beautiful
granddaughter Lana.

This book really is for Lana as she is the light of my
days and the reason I keep going.
She fuels my motivation to push through the dark
days, which in turn inspires me to bring my motivation
to all of you reading this.

Hi everyone

My name is GiGi, I am a recovering
alcoholic in sobriety almost 10 years.
I created this little book of Monday
thoughts to inspire you and show
you that Monday matters.
There's nothing to fear and
everything to gain from waking up
on a Monday Morning
Seizing the day leading to a brand
new week filled with adventures.
The aim of this book is to open it at
any page and read before you
crash into your day.
Hope you enjoy it as much as I
loved writing it.

Geraldine

I recall my past Mondays as periods of profound darkness, when I couldn't see how I would ever make it through the day.

Each morning I'd wake up gripped by fear, dreading the thought of repeating the same old routine all over again. Mundane tasks that I normally handled with ease took on monumental proportions in my mind, leaving me feeling defeated before the day had even begun.

My face wore an expression etched with dread. It was visible to those closest to me; they could sense that something was wrong.

In truth, the only thing wrong was my mindset and, unfortunately, my insecurities started to rub off on my family.

There's nothing more disheartening than seeing your mother consumed by fear, negativity, and anger. But this was the unfortunate result of my overactive imagination.

Ask yourself: Do you ever find yourself in this state, especially on Monday mornings?

When I decided to get my life on track, that was one of the first things I worked on: I swore that Mondays would never control me again. I was going to break free from the grip of Monday's gloom.

I came to realise that Monday was just a name assigned to one of the seven days of the week.
It wasn't inherently bad; it was just my perception of it that had made it seem bad.

I understood that if I could create this negative perception in my mind,
I also had the power to eliminate it.

And that's exactly what I did – I eliminated all the negative thoughts I'd been associating with Mondays.
I shifted my entire perspective. Now, I was in control of the day, not the other way around.
These days, Monday stands as one of the most beautiful days of the seven, filled with new starts, fresh opportunities, and excitement for the week ahead.
If I can make this transformation, I'm confident that you can too.

So, let's practise the idea that it's not the day of the week or the situation that determines our experience; it's our ability to approach life with a positive mindset from the moment we wake up.

Even on a Monday.

Monday mornings are often said to be
the hardest day of the week.

But why does this perception persist?
It's largely because the external world
constantly reinforces this idea.

However, our subconscious mind doesn't know about this
perception; it's a blank slate that
will believe anything we tell it.

This is why it's so important to set the tone for your day
when you first wake up by reassuring your mind
that today is going to be just fine.

Remember: what you feel in the early hours of Monday
morning is shared by millions of others waking up all around
the world.

These anxieties and uncertainties are not unique to you;
many have conquered them, and you can too.
Just take a deep, calming breath, and remember:
you've got this.

Let's keep in mind that most of our worries are essentially borrowed sufferings, and on Mondays, we tend to borrow more than usual.

Today, however, we won't dwell on those concerns. Instead, we'll exchange our anxiety for gratitude.

Trust me: this works every time.

If we make it a habit to begin our mornings by reflecting on what we're most grateful for, there will no longer be room for the notion of a 'bad day'.

Yes, there might be challenging moments, but they too will pass, making way for beautiful ones.

Always remember:
you have support, you are valued, and you are loved.

When is 'enough' ever truly enough?

If you start each day with dissatisfaction,
you will never be content.

Instead, be happy with what you have today,
and consider everything else
that comes as a delightful bonus.

If you always want more, I promise you will keep moving
the goalposts, leaving you unfulfilled each day.

So, be grateful for the simple fact that you woke up today,
for this day is a unique gift that will never come again.

The biggest mistake we make is assuming
that death lies in the future.

In reality, death is happening right now; every minute that
passes is a minute you will never get back.

The time that's passed already belongs to death.

I am 54 and I will never recover those years,
nor will I ever get to relive today.
What truly matters is the here and now.

It's vital to embrace and appreciate the present moment,
and to approach each day as if it were your last.

There will come a time in the future when you'll look back
and yearn to be the person you are today.

The way you talk to yourself has a profound impact on everything in your life.

If your self-talk is kind, positive, and reassuring, your day is more likely to unfold in the same way.

Conversely, if you're cruel, critical, and negative toward yourself, that negativity will tend to permeate your day.

It is essential, therefore, to pay close attention to the thoughts within your own mind, as that inner voice wields incredible power.

If someone at your workplace spoke to you the way you sometimes speak to yourself, you'd likely consider legal action!

Remember: the silent words you say to yourself can have a huge impact on your mental health.

We tend to endure greater suffering in our imaginations than we do in reality.
So, take a moment to pause and reflect.
Ask yourself: is the issue that's been consuming your thoughts

as dire in the outside world as it appears in your mind?
Stop overthinking and exaggerating things that often have straightforward solutions.

Say it out loud, confront it, and take action.

I assure you: when you wake up tomorrow morning, you won't even give it a second thought.

It's Monday, and it might be dark, cold, and raining outside.

The temptation to stay warm and snug beneath the covers is strong.

However, consider this: if you give in to that temptation, who would you be letting down today?

Your overthinking mind might struggle if you choose to stay in bed. After all, no one ever achieved much by hiding under the duvet. So, go ahead – throw the covers back, feel your feet on the ground, and know that there's a delicious cup of coffee waiting for you to start your day.

The bills that greeted you today are the very same ones you woke up to last Friday morning.
But, oddly, they didn't seem to bother you as much then.

After all, it was Friday, and the weekend lay ahead.
In reality, these bills haven't changed at all, but their impact feels magnified on a Monday.

I choose to view Mondays as a fresh beginning each week – a new day filled with fresh ideas and thoughts.
If those bills are playing on your mind, take action.

Make that phone call or reach out to someone who can help alleviate the financial burden.

Always remember: if money is your only worry today, then you are very blessed.

After all, this is one burden that can easily be lifted.

I understand that many of you are impacted by the repercussions of other people's actions.

However, amid all this mayhem, it's crucial to recognise that you're unwittingly surrendering a substantial amount of your time and energy to the problems caused by others.

The most powerful form of retaliation is choosing not to adopt the same behaviour as them.

Rather than investing your precious time in people who have hurt you, take a closer look at t
heir actions and who they are.

You'll probably discover that you wouldn't want to be them, as they often lead unhappy lives.

Refrain from seeking revenge or getting even. You've already won by rising above their negativity and choosing to be a better person.

Let's embrace 'Self-Compassion Monday'.

Self-compassion goes beyond self-care; it's not just applying
a face mask or taking a bath.

It delves deeper into truly being
compassionate toward yourself.

It's about not drifting through life in a state of numbness,
but instead acknowledging
that you're not perfect – yet you're doing your best.

It relies on you reminding yourself
of how important you are in the lives of others,
and aligning your self-perception with how others see you.

In a hundred years from now, the house you live in, the car you drive, and all your beloved family members won't be here. It's a sombre thought, but it's our reality.

We will all become distant memories – just pictures on walls – and, eventually, perhaps even less than that.
So, today, take a moment to look around you.

Observe your home, which you sometimes criticise because it's not big enough.

Examine your car or mode of transportation that may cost you a fortune to run.

Take a good look at your family, the same ones you might occasionally scold for making a mess.

And, in that moment, remind yourself that one day in the distant future, none of these things will exist.

However, they exist today, so give them the love and respect they truly deserve.

It's Monday – let's seize the day!

The most important part of your day is those first five minutes after waking. Instead of dragging yourself out of bed and stumbling into your day,
take those precious minutes to reflect and ask yourself:

How am I feeling right now?
How would I like to feel today?
How do I want my day to go?

What can I take control of to ensure a better day ahead?
These simple reflections can change everything about your morning and set a positive tone for the day ahead.

Try to keep the outside world at bay for
as long as possible,
as your internal world is
where the true magic happens.

Practise speaking to yourself with the same kindness and
respect that you'd expect from others.
Those words you use when addressing your inner self
play a fundamental role in shaping the person you are.

The language you employ influences your character, not
only in your eyes but also in the way you interact with
others.

This practice is crucial, especially on a Monday morning,
when a fresh start awaits.

Worries are the thieves of contentment.
It's important to recognise that the majority of what
we worry about lies beyond our control.

So, why squander precious time on things we can do
nothing about?

Choose what you will allow to worry you,
and take action where you can.

This allows you to become
in control of the outside world, which can lead to the
creation of a beautiful, serene inner world.

Before envy creeps in at the sight of others' wealth, remind yourself that, hidden behind their walls, there may be hidden struggles and sacrifices.

Wealth is undoubtedly a privilege, but it carries its own set of consequences.

A lot of affluent individuals are poor in happiness, because they find themselves always wanting more.

Living each day without appreciating what they have, and feeling that nothing excites them anymore, can lead to dangerous outcomes.

The key is to stay mindful, appreciating what you have today.

When faced with difficult decisions,
consider these questions:

Will the action you're about to take make you a better
person, or will it have a negative impact on you?

Will it impact your family for better or worse?

If it's something you inherently know is wrong,
will it inflict long-term harm on others?

Is the potential consequence worth the
choice you're about to make?

By contemplating these questions,
you'll likely find the answers you require.

No one wants to die,
not even those who seek entry to heaven.

Death is the destination we all inevitably reach,
a universal journey that no one has ever evaded.

It serves as nature's way to clear out
the old to create space for the new.
Someday, you'll become the 'old'.

Recognise that your time on Earth is finite.

Don't waste it by living someone else's life; shape your own
path and make the most of the time you have.

Upon waking, the realisation that
it's Monday will have crept in.

It's natural to feel sorry for yourself,
to wonder why you can't have every Monday off,
but let's take a moment to put things in perspective.

Turn on the news and watch it for just five minutes.
Now do you realise how lucky you are?
You have a safe haven with a roof over your head.

Many people across the globe are living in fear for their
lives, and you aren't among them.

Remind yourself of your blessings, embrace this privilege,
and make the most of the opportunities that come your way.

You don't need to have an opinion on everything.

Sometimes, it's perfectly fine to absorb
the information and then let it go.

You don't need to form an opinion or offer your input,
especially if expressing your thoughts could lead to
awkward or uncomfortable conversations,
and even arrogance.

We've all heard the saying, 'Show your true colours'.
So, make sure your colours shine bright today.

Suppressing your emotions doesn't serve you well.
It's essential to acknowledge and process your
emotions, accept them for what they are, and deal
with them in a healthy way.

Ignoring them can lead to an emotional burden that
becomes too heavy to bear.
So, stop ignoring them.

While you shouldn't be ruled by them, it's equally
important to learn how to cope with them effectively.

When you avoid dealing with your emotions, you risk
losing your balance and becoming powerless.

Remember: it's perfectly OK to express your emotions
and discuss your feelings with others.

Here we are, stepping into another Monday,
the start of a fresh new week.
Strangely, the to-do list might feel more daunting today,
even though it was probably the same on Friday,
and it didn't faze us then.

I believe it's our outlook on Mondays that
gives rise to these niggling fears.

Mondays mark the start of five days filled with work and
family responsibilities, and it can feel like an eternity until
the weekend arrives again.

It is crucial, therefore, to remind yourself that in just three
days, you'll once more be looking forward to Friday.

It's just a blink away.

We should always remind ourselves that Monday signifies the start of a whole new chapter, an opportunity to be productive and to get things done.

Life is fleeting, so let's not shy away from feeling powerful just because it's Monday.

Let's not squander this day; we can't relive it. Consider how many Mondays you've experienced in your lifetime. I've had around 3000.

Half of those we might not even remember because we were too young. As for the rest, we may have chosen to rush through them, pretending they don't exist.

Now, imagine telling a person who's near the end of their life that they have 3000 days left to live.

They would treasure every hour, cherishing the moments with their loved ones, not wanting to miss a single second. We should approach Mondays with the same perspective and appreciation for the time we have.

Hi, it's Monday!

Let's revisit our memory to-do list – those things we've been saying we really need to do – and put a plan in place, perhaps even creating a schedule to get started.

I'm not suggesting that everything has to be completed today, but mentally contemplating it and visualising how you'd feel once it's done can be enough to take that first step.

In life, it's all too easy to put things off for another day, but when that day never arrives, we end up carrying the burden of guilt for neglecting what needed to be done.

There's truly no greater feeling than accomplishing something we've been dreading and postponing.

And there's no better day to start than on this beautiful Monday.

Get it done – you know it's worth it!

Setting and achieving realistic goals is a worthwhile pursuit, especially when it comes to things like our weight or finances.

However, not every Monday has to start with a diet and a spreadsheet.

Mondays can be pressure-filled as it is, so it's OK to enjoy that bun and reconsider your options tomorrow.

Remember: balance is essential, and you still have the whole week ahead of you.

The meaning of life is created by our actions
Lots of little things will happen today that don't mean
anything , they are so insignificant to what really
matters, but we let them take over and dictate how
our day will go.

We put so much pressure on ourselves on Mondays
because we want a fresh start, We want everything to
go right, but the real question we must ask ourselves
when something changes our mood today is

Does this really matter?

Can this be fixed?

Did I cause this or was it the action of others?
How will this impact my life as a whole?

Let's sort it out.

This morning, ask yourself a simple question:
What is the most important thing in your life today?

It's on Mondays that we often magnify the significance
of the smaller things, such as dirty dishes, a pile of
washing, snide comments, a heavy workload, or
someone not pulling their weight.

These seemingly insignificant actions can lead us down
a regrettable path, where words are
spoken that can't be taken back.

They play on our minds and ruin our day.
But if we return to the initial question:

What is the most important thing in your life today?

You'll realise that none of these concerns
were part of your answer.

So why allow them to take on such importance when,
in the grand scheme of life, they mean nothing?

Don't dread waking up today.
Think about the alternative – not everyone was
granted the gift of another morning. Many would have
cherished the opportunity to have just one more day
on this earth. So, get up, be grateful,
and leave the complaints behind.

You'll find that the pity party is especially dull on a
Monday.

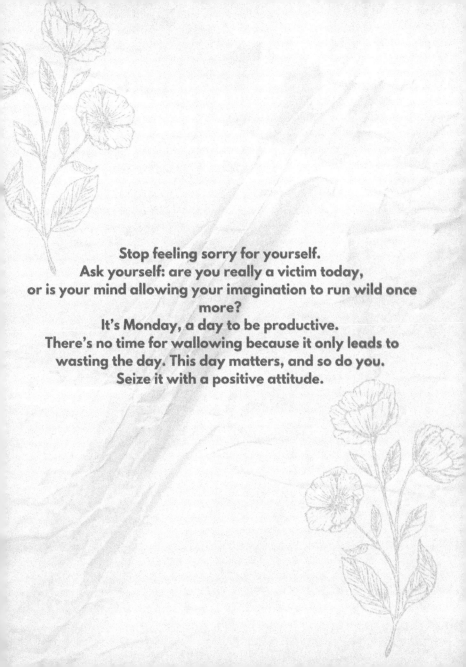

Stop feeling sorry for yourself.
Ask yourself: are you really a victim today,
or is your mind allowing your imagination to run wild once
more?
It's Monday, a day to be productive.
There's no time for wallowing because it only leads to
wasting the day. This day matters, and so do you.
Seize it with a positive attitude.

It's Monday – the perfect time to make amends.

So, swallow your pride, and try not to overthink it.
If something is weighing on your mind,
it needs to be addressed.

And what better day to do this than today?

Remember: forgiving someone who wronged us
is often more about granting ourselves peace and closure
than it is about the person we
harbour negative feelings towards.

Accepting things the way they are isn't a sign of failure; it's a breakthrough.

When you accept your life as it is today, you gain the insight needed to identify what needs to change. Merely complaining without taking action won't lead to personal growth.

Acceptance, along with understanding why you are the way you are, is the first step toward leading a happier life.

And what better day to embark on this journey of self-discovery than on a Monday?

Anxiety often runs high on Mondays,
and it can be challenging to
find the patience to work through it.

This impatience stems from the desire to get this day done
and dusted, with the hope that better times lie ahead.

But I'd like to pose a question: what's going to be different
tomorrow that you can't make happen today?

Instead of rushing through this day,
which is beautiful in its own way, strive to have more
patience and make the most of it.

There's a saying that goes:
'If you could only see yourself through my eyes, you would realise just how special you are.'

It's a reminder to be kind to yourself, to use empowering language, and to stop torturing yourself with self-doubt and negativity that only drains your inner spirit.

You need that spirit today to bring happiness not only into your own life but also into the lives of others.

On a Monday morning, you may wake up filled with concerns about the challenges you'll face during the day. But then, you shift your thoughts to your family and all the things they're having to go through.

Before you even get out of bed, the weight of the world can feel overwhelming.

It's as if not only your worries but also the worries of others have been placed, suddenly, on your shoulders.

With all this going on, how can your Monday be expected to go well?

In these moments, it's crucial to pause, take a breath, and remind yourself that it's not as bad as it may seem. The people you're worrying about are capable of managing their own lives, and your worries won't alter the course of their day.

Just remind yourself that you'll get through this day – because you always do.

You are the glue that holds everything together. So, approach the day with confidence, knowing you have the strength to get through it.

When you wake up today and feel consumed by the tasks and responsibilities ahead, take a moment to consider this:

Someday, when life takes an unexpected turn and things become truly challenging, you'll look back and give anything to be in the position you're in today.

Don't wish away the normal, even slightly boring, days. The future holds a mix of adventures, happiness, sadness, and challenges, and it's waiting for you.

Therefore, you should appreciate the here and now, because someday, it will look like perfection.

If the shoes you're stepping into today are ones you would rather not put on, just remember this: there are people out there who, right at this moment,
are facing a day like no other.

They've woken up to dreadful news that can't be altered, and they would give anything to trade places with you and kick off their own shoes.

Remember this when you feel sorry for yourself for no reason at all.

In life, almost everything can be fixed,
except for serious illness or death.

So, that thing you're fretting over?
It can be resolved.
It's never too late, and it's probably not as bad as you think.
Take a moment to say it out loud.

Is it really as bad as your busy mind is telling you?
Of course it isn't!
Now, get on with your day, and give it your best effort.

If you can change what's bothering you, take action.
If you can't, just let it go.

Life is too short to be bogged down
with unnecessary worries.

It's Monday once more,
and you're probably having a tough time getting up.
Well, nothing great is ever achieved by staying in bed.
So, get up, get dressed,
savour a cup of coffee, and ask yourself:

What makes me happy?

Within reason, surely you can inject
a little of that happiness into your day today?

Don't wait for someone else to bring you happiness;
everything you need is already within you.

Slow down, prioritise what's important today,
and focus on the present rather than worrying about what
may or may not be in the future.

Name one situation in which panicking helps.

Just name one.
The truth is, panic exacerbates every situation, making it
seem worse than it actually is.

Panic breeds fear, which in turn can lead to more mistakes.

So, on this Monday – or any other day – when things aren't
going as planned, remember this truth.

Panicking never helps.

Stop searching for the secret to a perfect life,
because it doesn't exist.

Instead, learn to be adaptable to whatever
life throws your way.

Life is inherently unpredictable
and can change in an instant.

That's why there's a saying,
'Aww well, that's life. What can you do?'

The truth is, you can do a lot if you stop looking for quick
fixes in a world filled with flaws.
Accept that today is no different from any other day.

It's what you make of it that determines the outcomes,
whether they're good or bad.

Adaptability and resilience are key to
navigating life's ups and downs.

Before heading out into the world today, take a moment to reflect on what might be bothering you.

Is it work?
Is it the commute?
Is it the family or the house?
Is it the people you have to spend time with?
Is it money?

There's usually one thing that can lead to frustration and bring your whole day down.

When this happens, it can make you feel like nothing in your life is going right.

However, you can just stop and ask yourself the question: what am I struggling with the most?

Say it out loud.
Now ask yourself: is this in my control?
Consider what you can do to minimise your feelings about it, or eliminate them altogether.

Remember: it's not everything.
It's not your whole life.
It's just one thing that you've allowed to take over and dictate the course of your day.
If you address it and manage it, you can regain control over your life.

It's important to take stock of all the things that
are going right in our lives.

Often, the things that don't bother us seem
insignificant, as if they don't matter.

However, in reality, these are the things
that truly make a difference.

We've already conquered them.
We might perceive them as irrelevant,
but they are the elements
that make our lives so much more bearable.

There will come a day when it will all make sense. So, if today doesn't go to plan, and you find yourself struggling against things that aren't going your way, take a moment to tell yourself that there may be a bigger plan at play.

Consider how often something that initially seemed disastrous in your life turned out to be a blessing. Instead of constantly going against the grain, try moving with it.

You might be genuinely surprised at the positive outcomes you experience.

Instead of waking up with a sense of 'poor me, I have to do it all over again,' consider the power you possess today and how you can use it.

You have the power to make someone smile.

To brighten someone's day.

To help someone feel important.
To show someone they are appreciated.

To ease someone's heavy burdens.

The power you have stepping into your Monday is priceless, and it's not all about you and how you feel.

It's much bigger than that; it's a force that can have a significant positive impact on the people around you.

It's Monday again, and you might wake up drea ding the day and yearning to have lots of money.

It's common to imagine how great it would be to be rich and famous, believing it would eliminate the Monday grind.

However, when you look beyond the wealth and trappings of someone else's success, consider what they may have traded for it, like their freedom.

Today, you have the freedom to live life on your own terms.

Don't waste it chasing something that could potentially take away the very freedom you cherish.

What's on your list today?

It's disheartening how much of our time we spend doing things just to impress others, not only fulfilling our obligations like work and family but also engaging in pointless actions solely to meet someone else's expectations.

Is it any wonder you feel like you can't cope? It's essential to stop chasing the validation of others and instead begin to chase your own self- worth.

Monday often feels like a day for impatience.
We want it to be over and done with, and anger tends to
rear its ugly head far more frequently.

They say that anger is a mild form of madness.
So, when you find yourself getting angry today,
it's crucial to pause before you react.

When speaking in anger, we can get carried away.
It overrides our judgement and makes it nearly impossible
to be patient or bite our tongues.

Oh, what this costs us – and what we come to regret!
Nearly every regret, mistake, or embarrassing moment –
whether it's personal or professional – shares a common
thread: somebody got carried away and wasn't thinking
beyond the next few seconds.

Remember this the next time you're confronted with a
frustrating situation.

The best way to approach Mondays is to be prepared.
Take some time out of your Sunday, a day when you
typically feel more relaxed, to do things that will make the
next morning much easier.

Lay out your clothes, prep dinner,
and make lunches in advance.

These small tasks take nothing out of us on a Sunday,
but can feel like a significant burden
if left to a Monday morning.

Plan and organise ahead of time,
and start your week with less stress.

Every time we say yes to something,
it means saying no to something else.

However, you can look at it like this:
Every time we say no to something today,
we can say yes to something that truly matters.

When you say yes to things that offer no real advantage to
you, someone or something
is not just taking up your time but also robbing you of the
time you could spend on family or work commitments.

For example, when you say yes to a night out or a party
you're not interested in, you're committing to giving up
valuable time that could be better spent elsewhere.

When you wake up on a Monday morning and anxiety takes over, causing your mind to venture into all sorts of dark places, it's essential to remind yourself of a few things.

You are a good person, and you haven't harmed anyone. In fact, the only person you are harming in this moment is yourself.

While many things may be beyond our control, our thoughts are very much within our control.

You have the ability to turn them around, to stop feeding the negative thoughts, to stop listening to them, and instead, start talking to them.

This way, you can reduce your anxiety and create a more positive outlook, even on a challenging Monday morning.

Saying 'no' is one of the hardest things in life.

It's such a small word but it has so much power, whether you're saying no to invitations, requests, or obligations.

Even more challenging can be saying no to time-consuming emotions like anger, resentment, and judgements.

If we're not careful, these emotions can consume our lives and rob us of precious time.

If you want to regain some of your time and be less busy, start saying, 'No, thank you, I just can't right now.' While it may offend some people, the more you say no to things you don't want to do, the more you can say yes to the things that truly matter to you.

It's Monday, and what a day to be alive!
Many didn't get the chance to wake up this morning,

so get out of bed and truly start living!

Don't merely go through the motions; make today matter.
This is the start of a new week, filled with fresh ideas and
endless possibilities.

Feel energised and use that energy to accomplish what
matters to you.

Imagine going to bed tonight
and being able to say,
'I achieved so much today, and I'm proud of myself.'

Embrace the potential of the day and make the most of the
start of this beautiful new week!

Some final thanks

My thanks is to you reading this.
Whether you are one of my loyal followers, one of my
Monday Club girls or just someone who
has picked up this book on a whim, I thank you.
By buying this book you have bought into my dream of
making the world a brighter and happier place.

A special thank you to my Monday Club.
The women who have supported me from the start.
Who joined my membership and made
my dreams a possibility.
I would not be here without you.

And lastly, a massive thank you to Sarah-Louise.
None of this would have been possible without her
expertise and help.

Love GiGi

Printed in Great Britain
by Amazon

32263082R00066